Exploring the Pioneer Trail

By SHAUNA GIBBY

Illustrated by CASEY NELSON

DESERET BOOK

Salt Lake City, Utah

Library of Congress Cataloging-in-Publication Data

Name: Gibby, Shauna, author.
Title: Exploring the pioneer trail : a flashlight discovery book / Shauna Gibby.
Description: Salt Lake City, Utah : Deseret Book, [2019]
Identifiers: LCCN 2018047214 | ISBN 9781629725758 (hardbound : alk. paper)
Subjects: LCSH: Mormon pioneers—West (U.S.)—History—Juvenile literature. | Frontier and pioneer life—West (U.S.)—Juvenile literature. | The Church of Jesus Christ of Latter-day Saints—History—Juvenile literature. | The Church of Jesus Christ of Latter-day Saints—History—Pictorial works. | LCGFT: Picture books.
Classification: LCC F593 .G43 2019 | DDC 289.3/3209—dc23
LC record available at https://lccn.loc.gov/2018047214

Printed in China
RR Donnelley, Shenzhen, Guangdong, China   1/2019
10 9 8 7 6 5 4 3 2 1

To Lee, Sarah, Elise, Kristi, and Candace.

Thanks for joining us on this journey!

—SG

To my parents, the Nelson family pioneers.

—CN

Leaving for a new home in the West
was an exciting adventure for
Latter-day Saint pioneer children.
They were heading to a place they called
Zion, where they could be with other
Saints. If you look closely at each page,
you will discover many things
the pioneers saw on their trek west.

Shine a flashlight behind the
color pages to see what is
hidden along the pioneer trail.

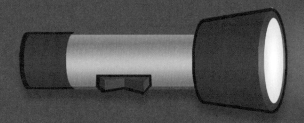

This pioneer family is getting ready to travel west.

Can you see what they've packed inside their wagon?

They have clothes, food, and supplies that they need for their journey, plus the items they'll need once they reach their new home.

Pa and Brother are putting the last barrel inside the wagon.

Can you see what is inside?

They've put their **best dishes** inside the barrel of dried beans to keep them from breaking on the bumpy trail.

The journey is underway!
The wagon is full, so the children
walk alongside it. A prairie dog
is watching them go past.

Where does he go when
he disappears?

The prairie dog lives with many others
in burrows under the ground.

The company captain helps the pioneers find their way, be safe, and do what is right.

What does he carry on his horse?

He keeps his rifle close by to protect the pioneers and to hunt for food. He uses the scriptures to read with the pioneers at night.

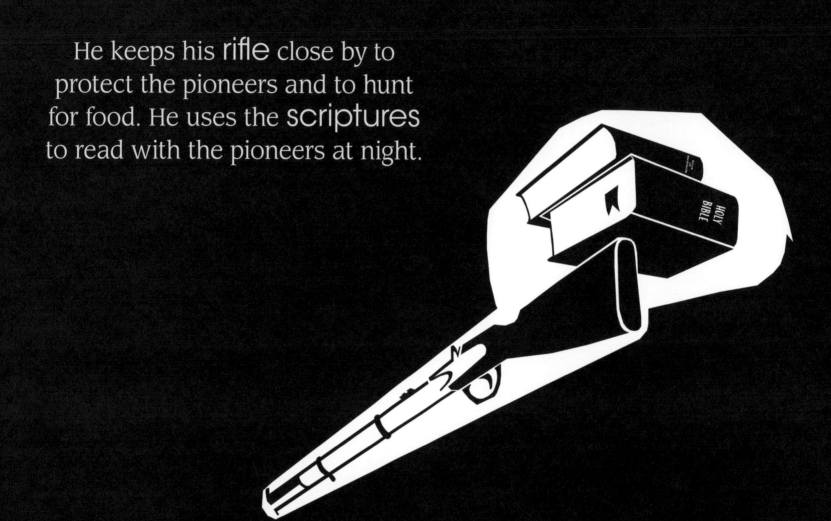

When the pioneers stop each evening, they gather their wagons into a large circle.

What is inside the circle?

They use the protected area
inside the wagon circle to build
campfires and cook dinner.
Sometimes they sing and dance.

After the bugle sounds, it is time for evening prayer and lights out. Sometimes during the night there are strange noises outside of camp.

What is making that howling noise?

They are wolves. Wolves hunt at night and their howls are how they communicate with each other.

Sometimes the children walk ahead of the wagons so they can have time to play.

What game are they playing?

This game is called "Shadow Tag." The player who is "It" tries to step on the other children's shadows. Pioneer children also like to play Run, Sheepie, Run; Anti-I-Over; and Hide and Seek.

After seeing nothing but flat prairie for many days, the pioneers are happy to see large trees.

What is behind the trees?

It's a river. The pioneers can fill their water barrels, wash their clothes, and enjoy fish for dinner.

Some of the rivers are too deep to walk through.

How do the pioneers get to the other side?

They build a raft out of logs
and float the wagons across
one or two at a time. These
rafts are called ferries.

The children have the job of gathering sticks and buffalo chips to burn in their fires, but they need to be careful. There is a warning noise telling the children not to go near this patch of grass.

What is in the grass?

It's a **rattlesnake!** The noise is made by the rattle at the end of its tail. When the rattlesnake is alarmed, it will create a rattling sound to warn the intruder to stay away.

Along the way the pioneers pass a large fort where soldiers live.

Do you know what is inside the fort?

There are walkways around the top of the walls so the soldiers can see who is approaching. There are also cabins for the soldiers.

Sometimes the pioneers pass
Native American villages.

What is inside the tepee?

The pioneer is **trading** with a Native American. He gives them clothes, food, and knives to get buffalo robes and moccasins.

There is a large rounded rock formation near the trail. It is called Independence Rock. It is a landmark that can be seen for miles.

Can you see what is on the rock?

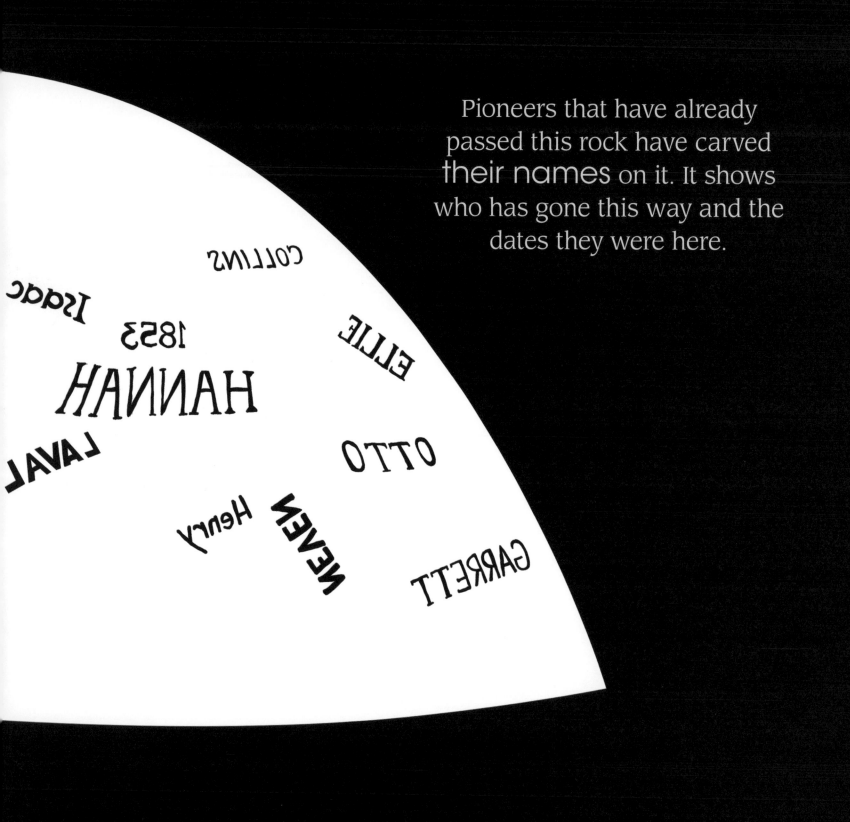

Pioneers that have already passed this rock have carved **their names** on it. It shows who has gone this way and the dates they were here.

The pioneers are grateful they have nearly reached their destination.

Do you know where they are going?

Salt Lake City is in the valley below. Here the pioneers will build homes, plant crops, and live with their families in peace. They will build a temple where they can be sealed together as families.

More than 70,000 Latter-day Saint pioneers crossed the plains with wagons and handcarts. They helped settle many towns in Utah and other western states